LEADLIGHTS
FOR LAMPSHADES
AND MIRRORS

LEADLIGHTS FOR LAMPSHADES AND MIRRORS

Kim Fowler

Kangaroo Press

This book is dedicated to Luke and Arlie,
my special boys

Acknowledgments
Thanks to all my friends, family and students for their encouragement
and faith in this book. A big thanks to Bill Mahoney of Leadlights of
Mogo (South Coast of NSW), an excellent and methodical teacher.
Special thanks to Anne Byrne for her expertise on the keyboard, and
the pleasure of working with her (we made a great team!) and most of
all thanks to the Lord Jesus, my inspiration and friend.

First published in 1995 by Kangaroo Press Pty Ltd
Reprinted in 1995
3 Whitehall Road Kenthurst NSW 2158
PO Box 6125 Dural Delivery Centre NSW 2158
Printed in Hong Kong through Colorcraft Ltd

ISBN 0 86417 672 4

Contents

Introduction

The idea of publishing this book was originally conceived while I was teaching. Since then, my students and friends have encouraged me. I discovered during my classes that there seemed to be a call for another book to inspire leadlighters—one which dealt with mirrors, lampshades and coachlamps. This book contains patterns for thirty of the most popular designs from my studio, featuring a wide variety of themes. I have included extra trade tips to help you achieve a more professionally finished product, but I have not gone into depth concerning techniques of leadlighting and copperfoiling as there are numerous excellent books which cover this area.

The inclusion of a piece of leadlighting in any room adds warmth, character and interest, regardless of the decor (and I am definitely not biased!).

LAMPS

Lampshade techniques and tips

Keeping these techniques and tips in mind will help you achieve a more professional finish to your work.

Use the variations and the colour in the glass to make your lampshade more interesting. Different textures of glass add another dimension. Choose the shape that you prefer, or that best suits your base; within that shape you can design your own lampshades to suit a particular room, the colours in the room, the period or any decor.

Tip: Hold the glass in front of a normal household lightbulb to see its true colours, rather than a fluorescent light.

1. Cutting When cutting out the lamp, be as accurate as possible, bearing in mind that the outside edge of each panel is just inside the black line on the pattern, and stay straight. If you aren't accurate, you will find when you place pieces of glass in the jig that the sides are uneven, the pieces are too small or too big. If the pieces are too big they won't fit in the jig, if too small they will put the lampshade out of shape or leave you with large gaps between the seams. Accuracy always pays—your lamp will be symmetrical and well balanced.

Tip: When breaking narrow pieces of glass, use two pairs of pliers—one to hold the narrow piece and the other to break. It works wonders.

2. Grinding Grind and number each piece of glass corresponding to the numbered pattern, dry and wipe clean.

3. Foil I like to use 5 mm ($\frac{3}{16}$'') copperfoil (use black-backed for transparent glass). Use 6 mm ($\frac{7}{32}$'') or 7 mm ($\frac{1}{4}$'') foil with thicker glass. Centre glass on foil, run foil around the edge, overlap and tear or cut off. Press sides over and burnish with a lathekin or pen. When the foil doesn't stick the most common causes are the glass not being clean or high atmospheric humidity.

4. Place the pattern on the bench and nail wooden bats just on the outside of the two vertical lines of the panel. Place your glass within the jig, adjusting if necessary.

5. Soldering techniques   Paint flux on all foil in sight *except the two vertical outside edges*. Then solder; don't play around in one area of your panel for too long or on pieces that are thin (tips of leaves, etc.) as the glass can get too hot and crack—disappointing when you're getting somewhere fast. Touch the glass to see if it is too hot. Move to the other end of the panel and go back when the glass has cooled a little.

Solder a raised bead (a smooth rounded seam) on the outside of the panel, raising it by adding more solder, then turn over and flat solder on the inside. As you get to know your soldering iron, your work will become neater. Don't despair at your work, because I guarantee as time goes by soldering will become second nature. *Don't* drag the iron quickly along the surface of your seam, that makes it messy. Don't fear soldering but approach it with a sure hand.

To smooth out lumpy areas press iron down (to the glass) and up firmly. You can also run the soldering iron along the seams, but make sure the tip of the iron is touching the glass and foil.

If the tip of the iron is pitted or damaged it will tear the foil. Always keep the tip filed smooth and tinned.

Have a container of water nearby to cool the iron by dipping the end of the tip into it.

If there is too much solder at one point, press iron down firmly, take it up quickly and flick it so the excess drops off. Soldering will never be perfect, so if you are getting frustrated, go for a walk or have a cup of tea or both!

Solder all panels, wash with whiting or dish-washing liquid, rub numbers off with towelling, and dry. If you don't finish soldering all the panels by the end of the day, wash the ones that you have finished. Never leave flux on glass overnight as it will leave stains on the glass—always wash flux off.

Soldering a lamp together, cleaning and applying patina should be done over one or two days at the most, as the patina will take more evenly.

Note: I use Bakers Solder Fluid for all soldering (copper and lead) except around mirror joints, where tallow candle is used. I use 60–40 solder for all soldering.

6. Forming a cone   Place panels side by side leaving 1 mm between panels. (When working with lampshades with only 4 to 6 panels, leave 1–2 mm space so the panels won't be too tight when pulled up to the cone position.) Apply heaps of masking tape or sticky tape, which I find works even better. Overlap the tape with a ring going around the top and bottom (see Figures 1 and 2). Don't scrimp on the tape—better to overdo it than underdo it, as the lamp could collapse and you would find yourself starting again. So rule 1: make

Figure 1

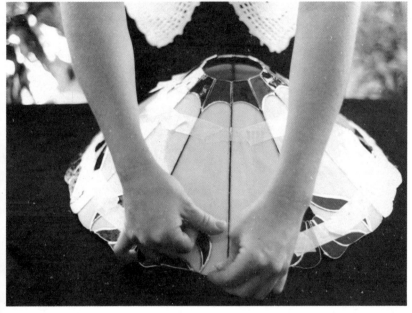

Figure 2

sure glass is very clean and don't scrimp on tape. In humid climates foil and cone indoors or near fans.

Pulling lamp towards your body and letting the edge of it lean against you, pull the lamp up so that edges meet, and secure with tape. Check to see that panels are meeting correctly at top and bottom of all seams and that the edges are sitting flat on the table. Flux all top and bottom joins and tack-solder.

7. Positioning the vase cap   Sit the vase cap on top of the lamp, check to see that it is sitting straight and centred, and tack-solder to the seams (see Figure 3 on the next page). This gives the lamp a lot of strength. Try different caps to see which suits best. If there

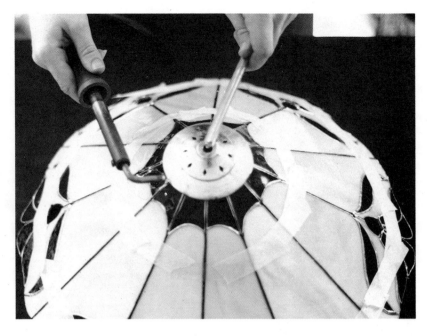

Figure 3

are big gaps between the rim and the lamp just solder the cap at the seams to start with. Later on, when you turn the lamp over to do the inside seams, apply masking tape over the gaps between the cap and the glass panels, so when you finish soldering the cap on the outside the solder will not drip through. Usually with 6-sided or 8-sided caps I only solder the seams to the cap anyway. When the wire is soldered around at the bottom the lampshade will be strong enough—use your judgment.

Note: Some caps will take patina straight away and go black; if not, you'll need to tin the cap. Apply flux, rubbing in well, take a *little* solder and start spreading it around, working it in a circular motion. If it's streaky or lumpy, too much solder has been applied (see Soldering techniques). Do this *before* tacking the cap to the top of the lamp.

8. Soldering seams   Solder blobs of solder all the way down each seam (see Figure 4). If the solder begins to run, move further down the seam and come back later. Keep on applying solder until you can't see any daylight between seams. This means that when you smooth the solder out, you won't have to apply much more to achieve a nice rounded beaded seam.

Turn the lamp over and lay it on the bench, then solder the seam that is closest to the bench. Solder all seams, rotating the lamp as you go. When they are done, turn lamp over.

Hold the lamp so that the seam you are working on is horizontal to the bench (see Figure 5). Hold the lamp very still and finish off the seam by making a nice rounded bead (see Soldering techniques). When all seams are beaded, place the lamp on a folded towel or some thick sponge and run copper wire around the bottom (see Figure 6). Stretch the wire over your flux brush to remove any kinks,

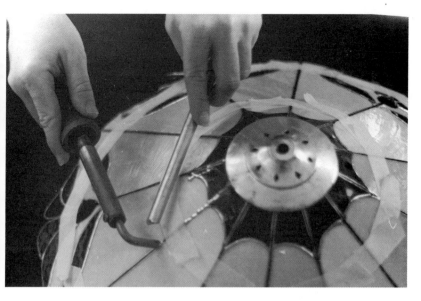

Figure 4

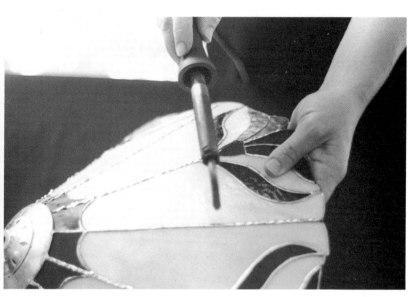

Figure 5

Figure 6

tack-solder and continue to press the wire against the rim of the lamp, tacking as you go, and overlapping at the end. Cut with leadcutters, then go back around and bead-solder.

9. Cleaning and polishing   Clean the lamp with whiting, water and a piece of towelling. Rinse. (I do this out on the grass with a running hose.) Patina with a paint brush, trying not to let any patina touch the glass as it leaves faint marks. I continue to run water over the lamp as I go. Patina inside as well. Clean patina off with whiting and water, then towel dry. Apply stove-black polish with a toothbrush, paying attention to all soldered area, and polish with a soft brush. Sometimes it's a little hard to remove all the polish from the glass—you might need to dampen a cloth and wipe the glass only—then finito. Congratulations! What a lovely lamp you have made.

10. Repairing   If you break a piece of glass during construction of your lampshade it's easier to repair it once the lamp is completed. These instructions apply to any broken glass in a foiled project. Score the surface of the broken piece, criss-crossing it in all directions, then with safety glasses on, tap the underside of the glass with the end of your glass cutter. The glass will crack and fly about (hence the safety glasses). Remove as much broken glass with pliers or tweezers as you can. Heat up the soldering iron, apply flux to the solder which was around the broken piece and melt the solder. Find the end of the piece of foil which was around the broken glass and pull the foil away from the lamp at the same time. Cut a new piece of glass and replace.

Note: Because of the distortions which can occur during photocopying, always check your patterns before cutting. The outside lines of an individual panel are the most important — they must be symmetrical.

Federation lily lamp

Illustrated on page 17

12 panels (6 repeats). This lamp uses the same design reversed in each pair of panels. Cut 6 panels, then reverse the pattern (face down) and cut 6 more.

Lamp height 175 mm (nearly 7″)

Diameter 460 mm (18″)

Base: Lady Diana LB316 or LB317

Tips: Cut centre piece of flower to fit after lamp is completely assembled

Enlarge pattern by 133%
(3 cm = 4 cm; 1½″ = 2″)

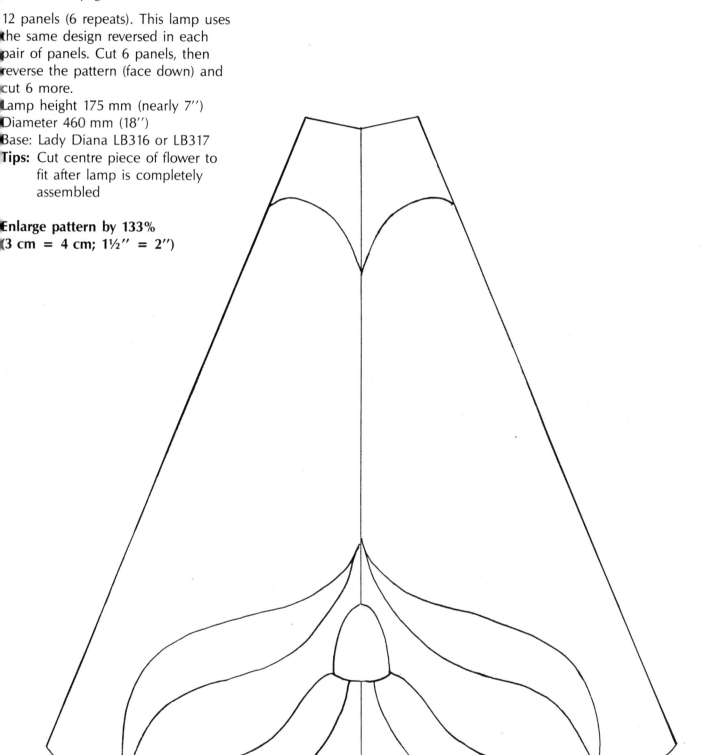

Bevelled federation lamp

Illustrated on page 17

12 sides—cut 4 of each piece of red,
blue and green
Glass: Red and green Kokomo and
dark blue Antique
12 bevels 2.5 cm × 2.5 cm (1″ × 1″)
Tips: Accurate cutting
     Solder bottom row in jig
     Bead around bottom

Pattern actual size

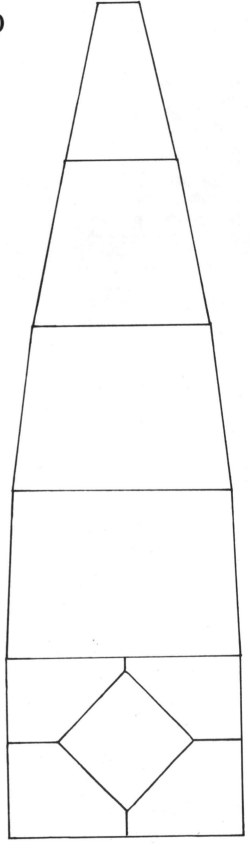

Lotus lamp

Illustrated on page 17

8 panels
Lamp height 240 mm (9$\frac{1}{2}$″)
Diameter 430 mm (17″)
Base: LB325
Tips: Kokomo background glass and
      dark blue Antique

**Enlarge pattern by 125%
(4 cm = 5 cm; 2″ = 2$\frac{1}{2}$″)**

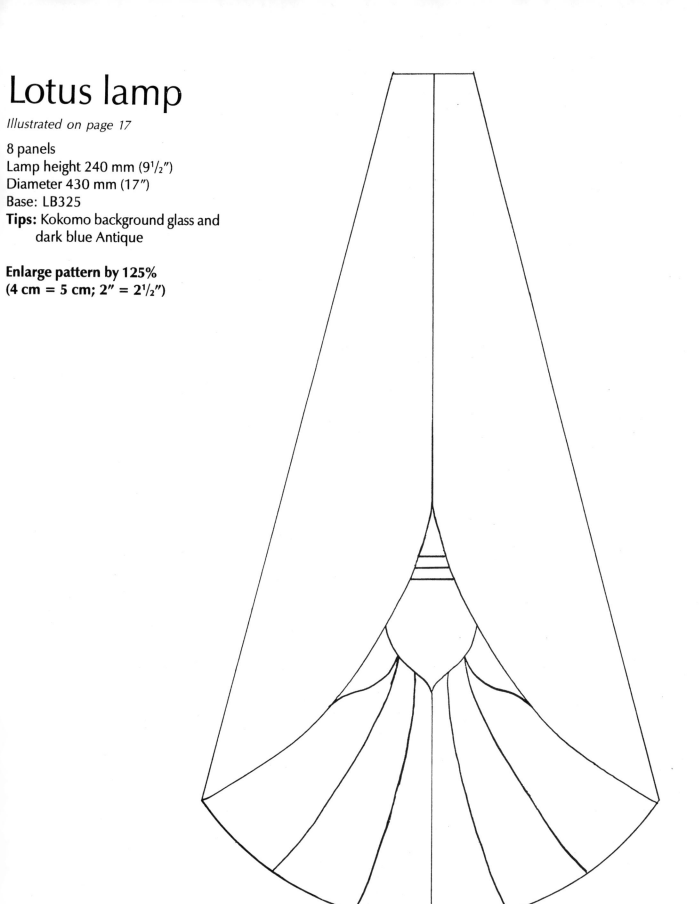

Blue and white floral lamp

Illustrated on page 17

12 panels
Lamp height 172 mm (6¾'')
Diameter 453 mm (almost 18'')
Base: LB325
Tips: Easy

Pattern actual size

Federation lily lamp (page 13)

Bevelled federation lamp (page 14)

Lotus lamp (page 15)

Blue and white floral lamp (page 16)

Petite roses lamp (page 19)

Sunflower lamp (page 20)

Gentleman's desk lamp (page 21)

Art Nouveau butterfly lamp (page 22)

18

Petite roses lamp

Illustrated on page 18

12 panels
Lamp height 197 mm (7¾'')
Diameter 390 mm (15⅜'')
Base: LB342
Tips: Cut 4 of panel A, 8 of panel B
and 12 of panel C.

Pattern actual size

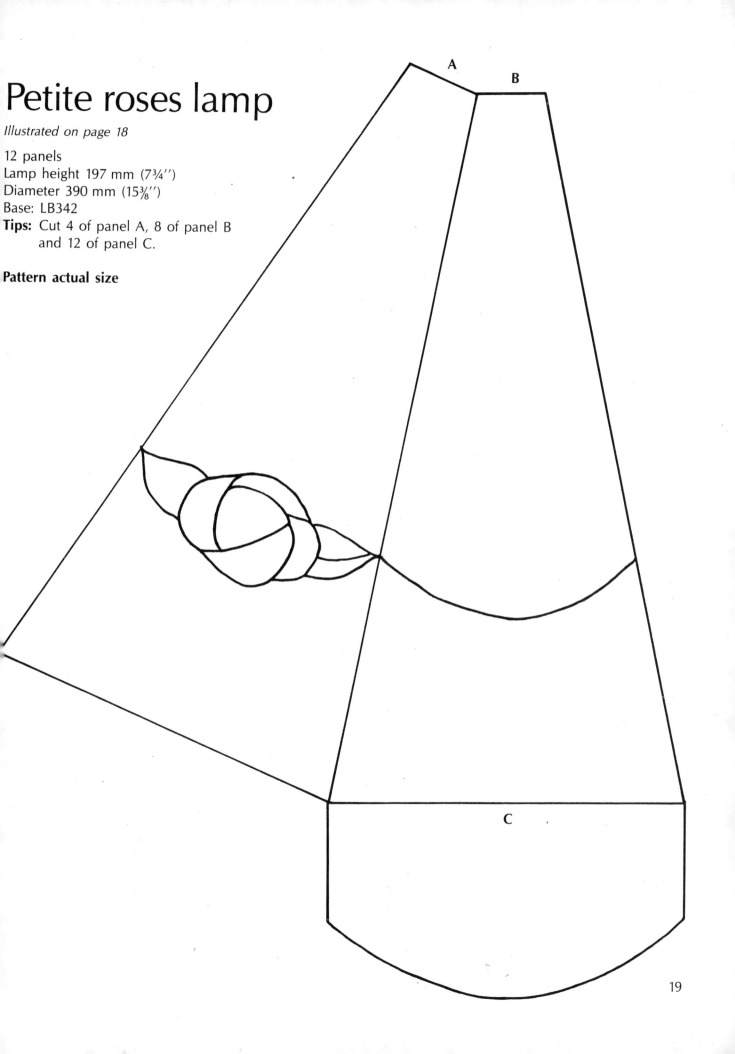

Sunflower lamp

Illustrated on page 18

4 sides
Base: LB313
Tips: Every girl should have one!
Definitely an eyecatcher

Pattern actual size

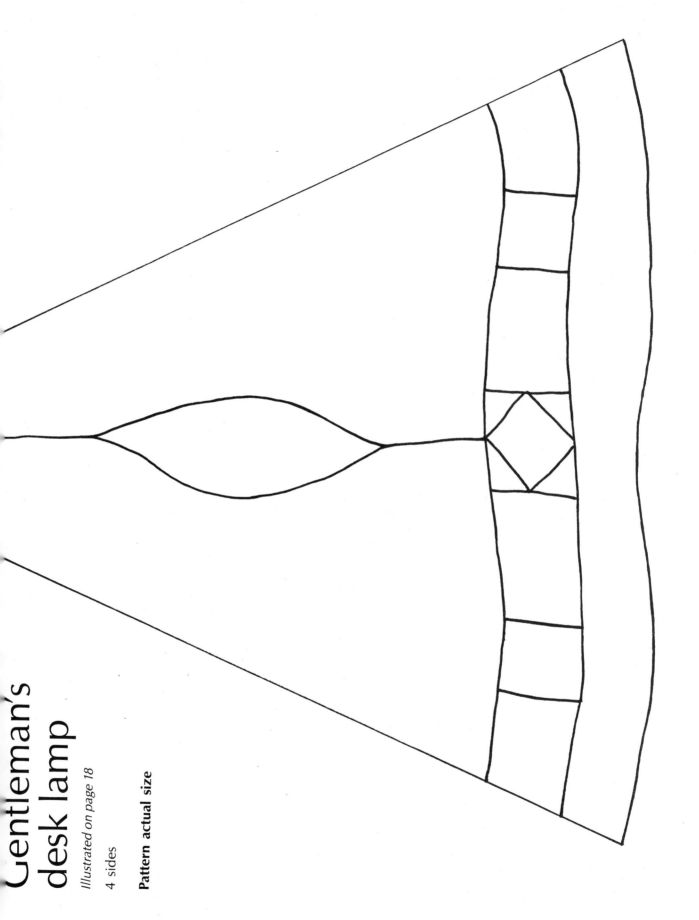

Gentleman's desk lamp

Illustrated on page 18

4 sides

Pattern actual size

Art Nouveau butterfly lamp

Illustrated on page 18

12 panels—cut 6 each of panels A
and B. This lamp uses the same
design reversed in panels A and B.
Cut 6 panels (A), then reverse the
pattern (face down) and cut 6 panels
(B).
Lamp height 178 mm (7″)
Diameter 463 mm (18¼″)
Base: LB316 or LB317

Enlarge pattern by 133%
(3 cm = 4 cm; 1½″ = 2″)

Tips: Some difficult pieces in the
background glass.
Use small grinding head for
space for jewels.
Cut body and head to fit in
one piece after lamp is
completely assembled.
This is also lovely with only
ten panels.

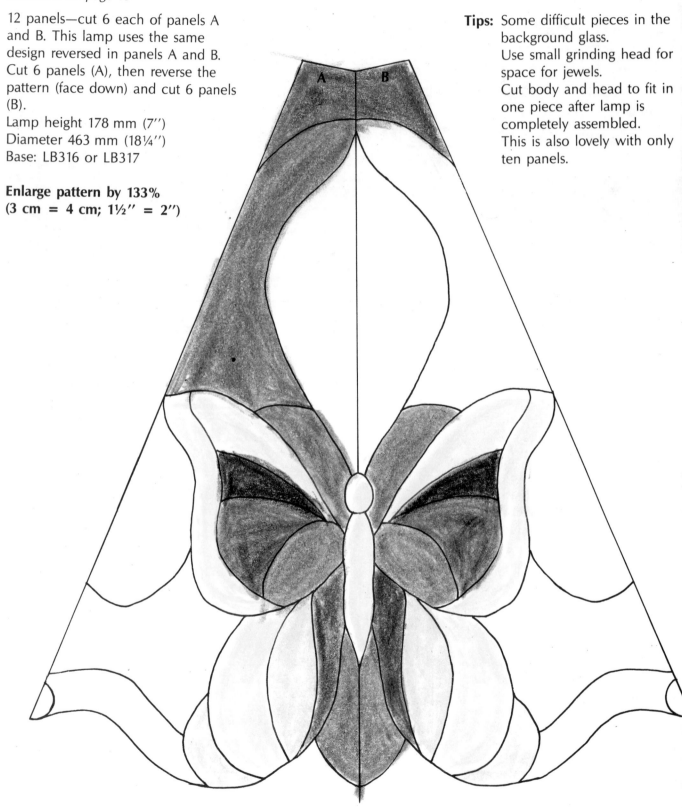

Belle cyclamen lamp

Illustrated on page 35

12 sides
Lamp height 230 mm (9″)
Diameter 430 mm (17″)
Base: LB1017

Tips: Accurate cutting otherwise
you'll have big gaps around
middle pieces.
Also looks great used as a
hanging light.

Pattern actual size

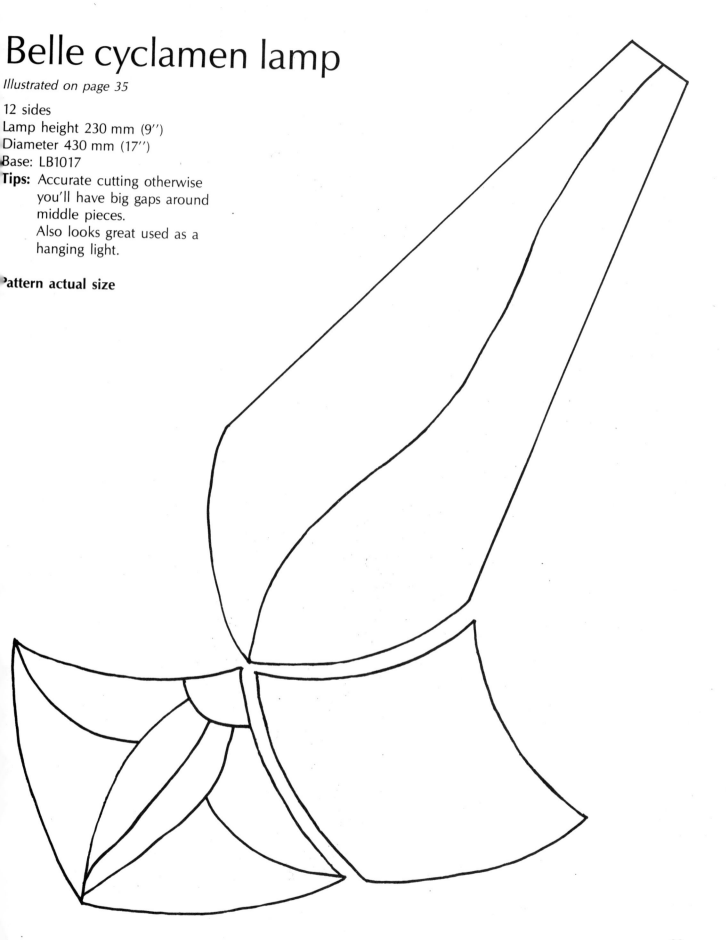

Blue shell lamp

Illustrated on page 35

6 unmarked scallop shells (or
similar) about 40 mm (1½'') long
6 sides—cut 6 of skirt
Lamp height 145 mm (5¾'')
Diameter 195 mm (7¾'')

Tips: Clean and foil shells, burnish.
Centre shell on glass and mark
around it.
Cut and grind to snugly fit
around shell. Solder shells in
place.
Use spider cap in place of
vase cap for a different effect.

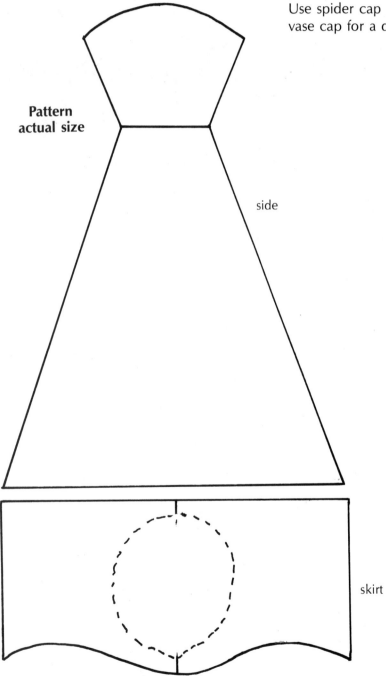

**Pattern
actual size**

side

skirt

join

Blue butterfly fan lamp

Illustrated on page 35

Check bottom measurements to fit your base. I used clear hammered glass for the pattern parts marked C.

Enlarge pattern by 133%
(3 cm = 4 cm; 1½″ = 2″)

join

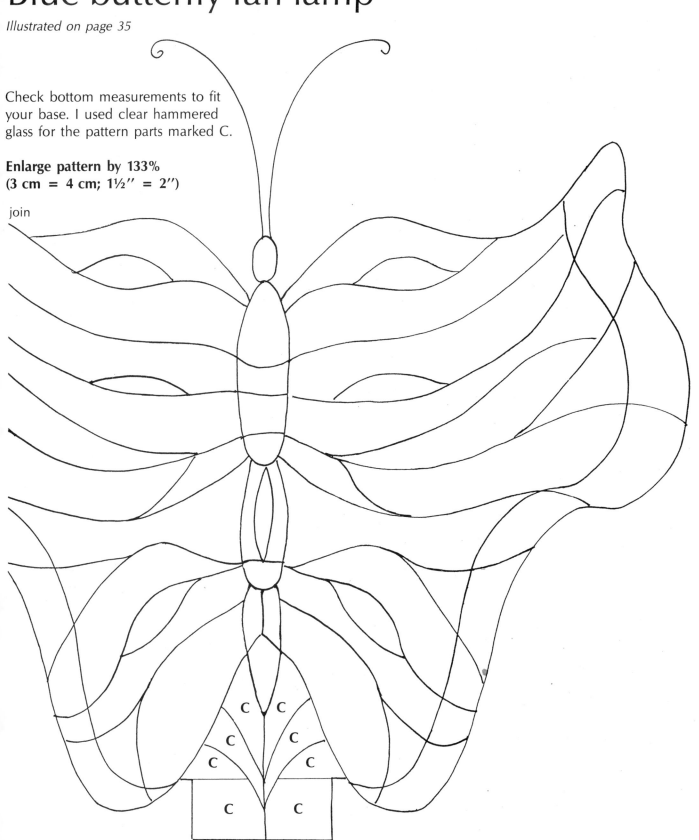

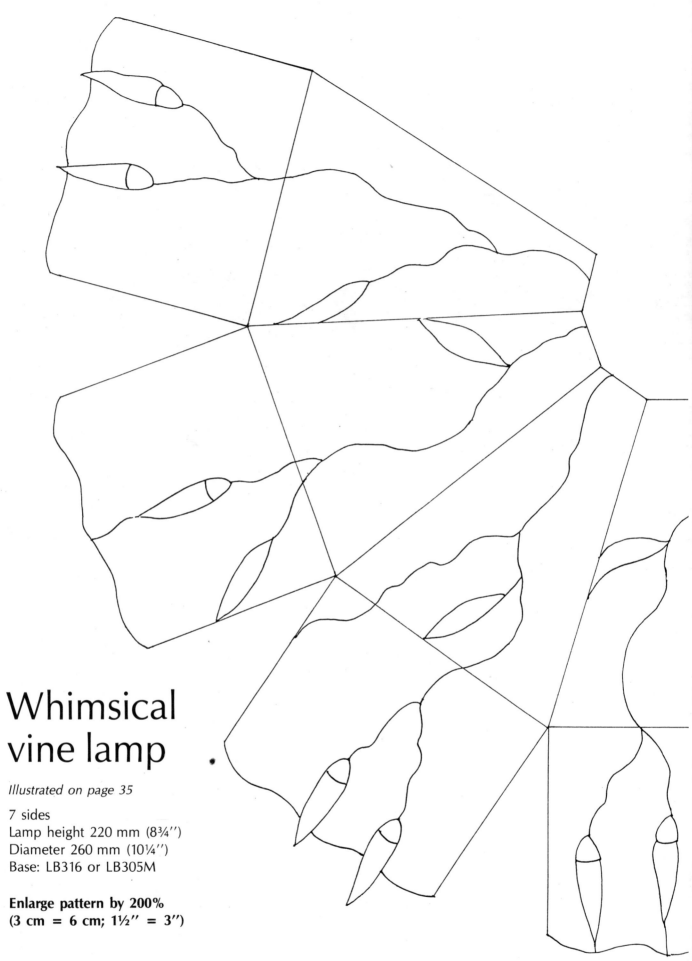

Whimsical
vine lamp

Illustrated on page 35

7 sides
Lamp height 220 mm (8¾")
Diameter 260 mm (10¼")
Base: LB316 or LB305M

**Enlarge pattern by 200%
(3 cm = 6 cm; 1½" = 3")**

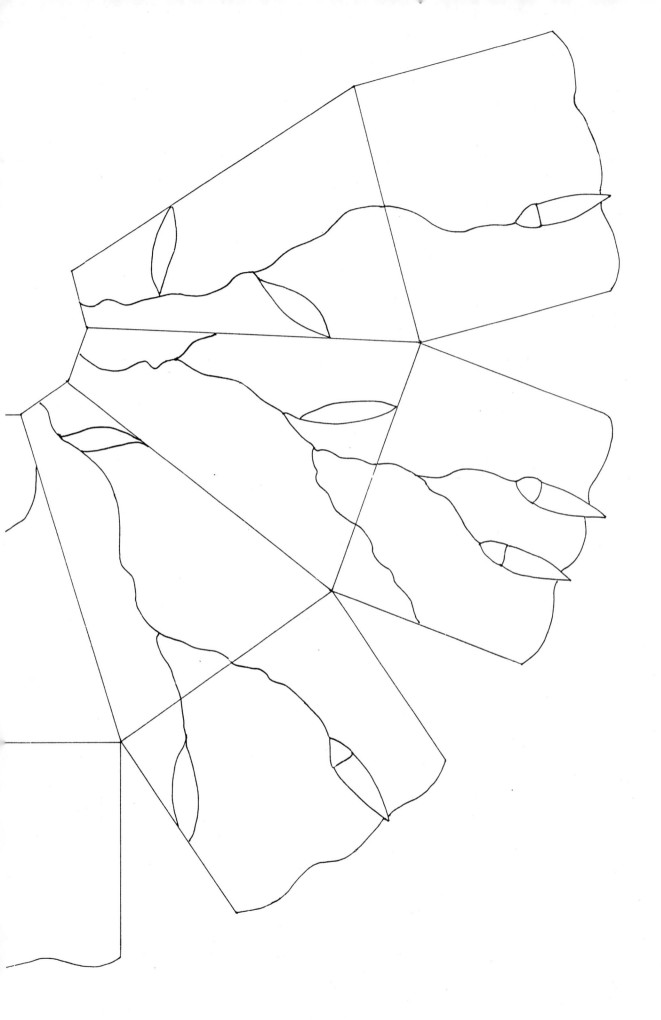

Australian natives lamp

Illustrated on page 36

4 sides
Lamp height 320 mm (12½'')
Diameter 405 mm (16'')
Base: LB315

A celebration of Australian wild
flowers, including some well known
and others less documented — wild
potato, boronia and Tasmanian
leatherwood.

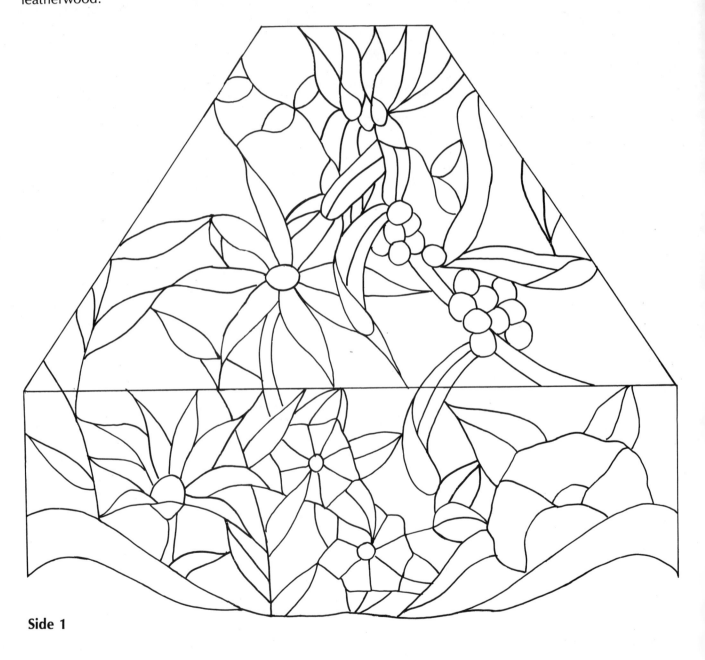

Side 1

I had the vase cap specially made
by Bains Harding, but making the
lamp with a crown would avoid the
problem.
This also makes a lovely hanging
lamp — over a big kitchen table it
looks fantastic.

Enlarge patterns by 225%
(3 cm = 6.75 cm; 2″ = 4½″)

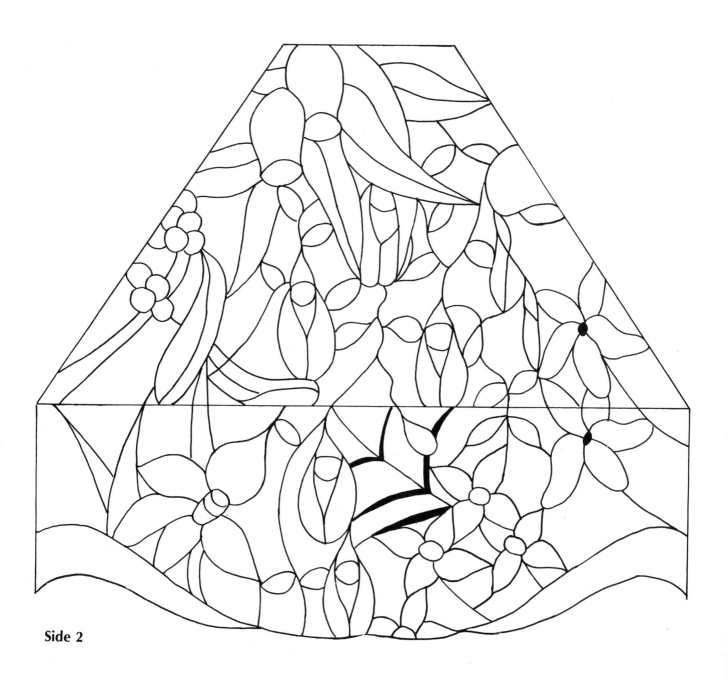

Side 2

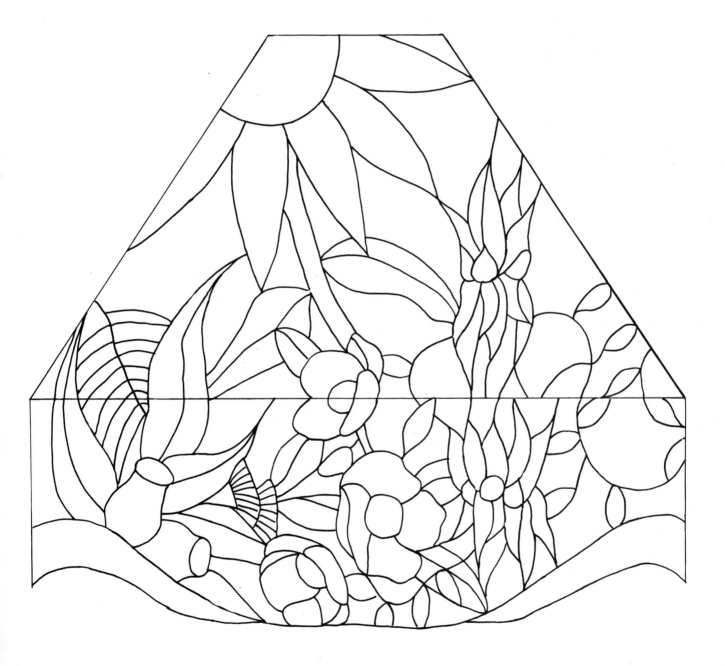

Arum lily fan lamp

Illustrated on page 36

Complete fan, and wash it with whiting.
Make up the lilies, then tack-solder them to the fan.
Cut out stamens and solder on top of lilies. Solder a piece of U6 lead to the bottom of the fan and cut flush. Patina the whole fan and the lilies, polish, and slide into the base so that the fan sits upright. You might have to leave a blob of solder in a few places on the back of the fan—experiment.

Enlarge pattern by 125%
(4 cm = 5 cm; 2″ = 2½″)

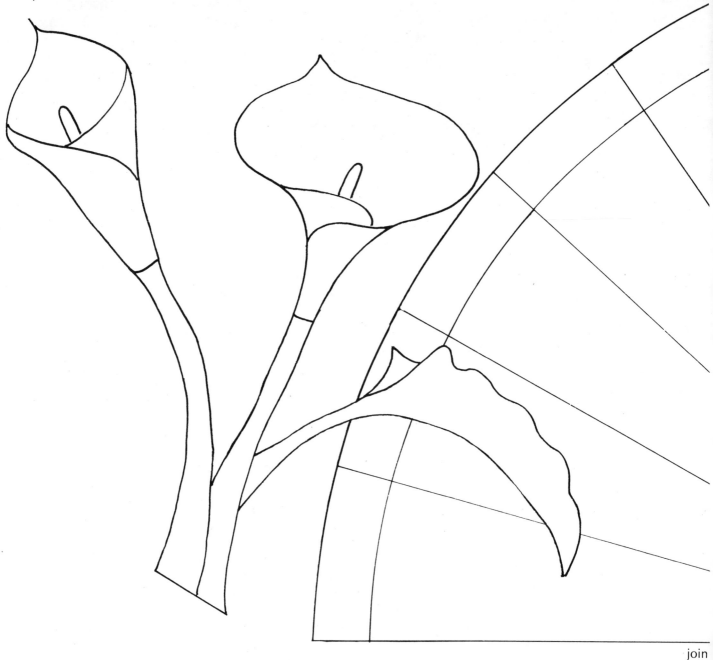

join

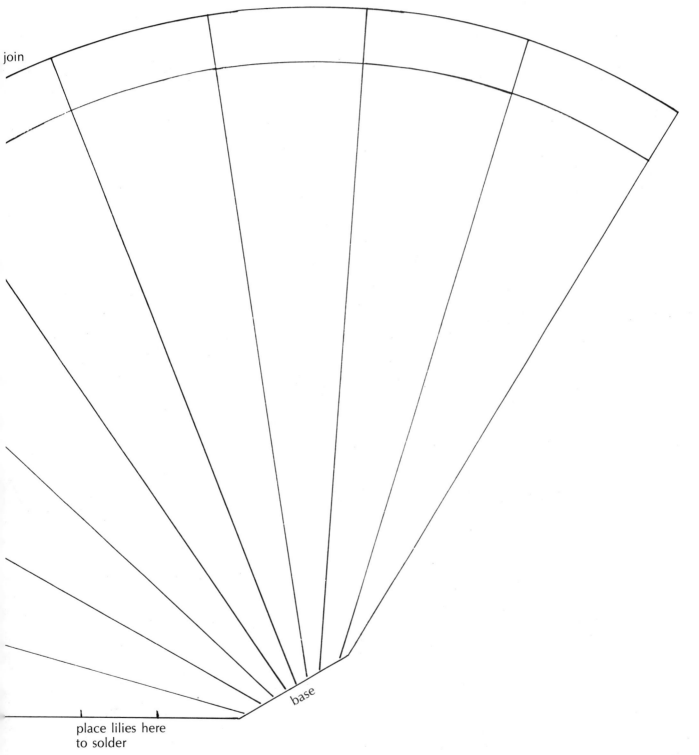

join

base

place lilies here
to solder

Fuchsia lamp

Illustrated on page 45

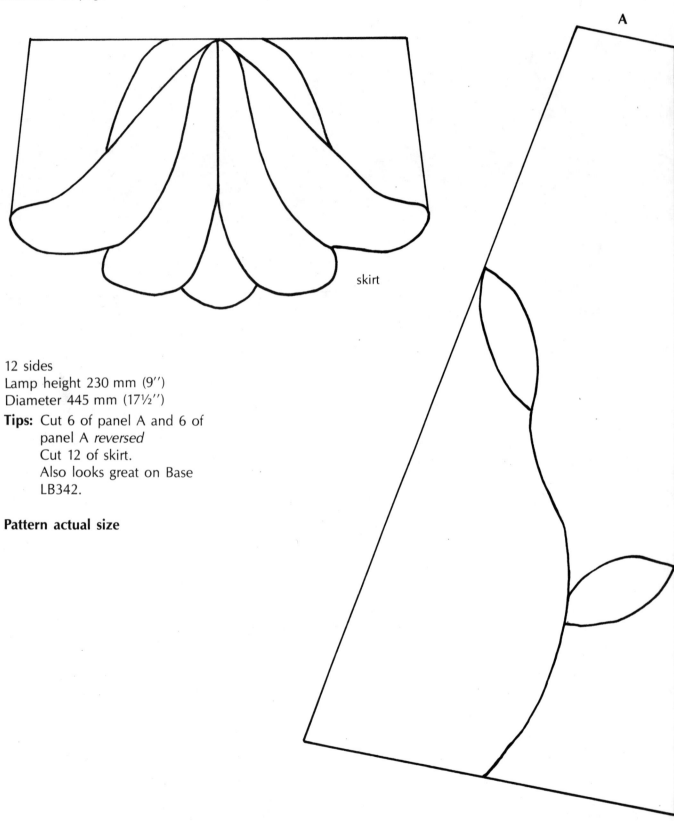

skirt

A

12 sides
Lamp height 230 mm (9″)
Diameter 445 mm (17½″)

Tips: Cut 6 of panel A and 6 of
panel A *reversed*
Cut 12 of skirt.
Also looks great on Base
LB342.

Pattern actual size

Belle cyclamen lamp (page 23)

Blue shell lamp (page 24)

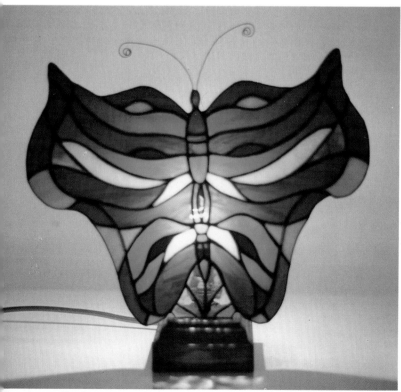

Blue butterfly fan lamp (page 25)

Whimsical vine lamp (page 26)

Two views of the Australian natives lampshade (pages 28–31)

Arum lily fan lamp (page 32)

Old-fashioned butterfly lamp

Illustrated on page 45

Hanging lamp
8 sides
Lamp height 280 mm (11″)
Diameter 360 mm (14″)

Enlarge pattern by 133%
(3 cm = 4 cm; 1½″ = 2″)

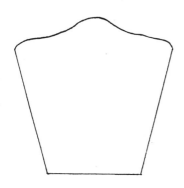

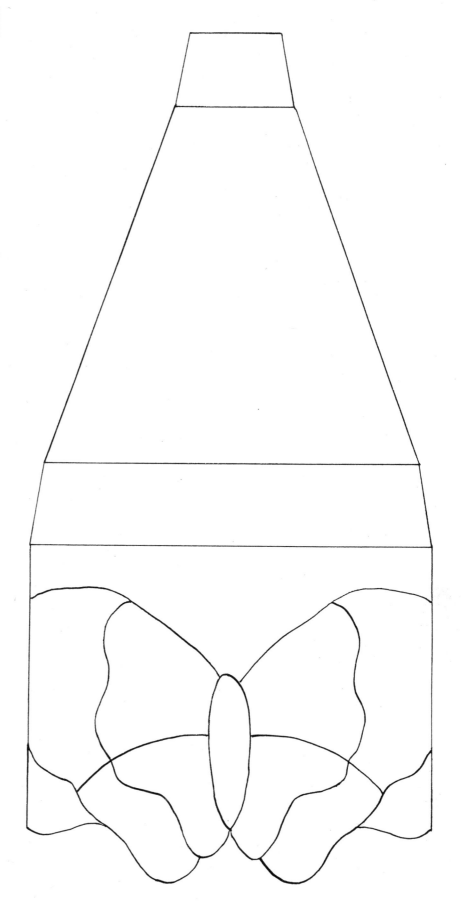

Kitchen fan lamp

This was sold and now lives in Brisbane. Unfortunately I didn't take a photo. It looked excellent as the word 'kitchen' was in black and white glass, set off by the yellow pineapple, lime-green Bullseye leaves, Red Spectrum apple and of course the proverbial blue and white jug. The background was amber and blue/white Kokomo glass, which gives off a lovely glow. Adjust the bottom piece to suit your own base.

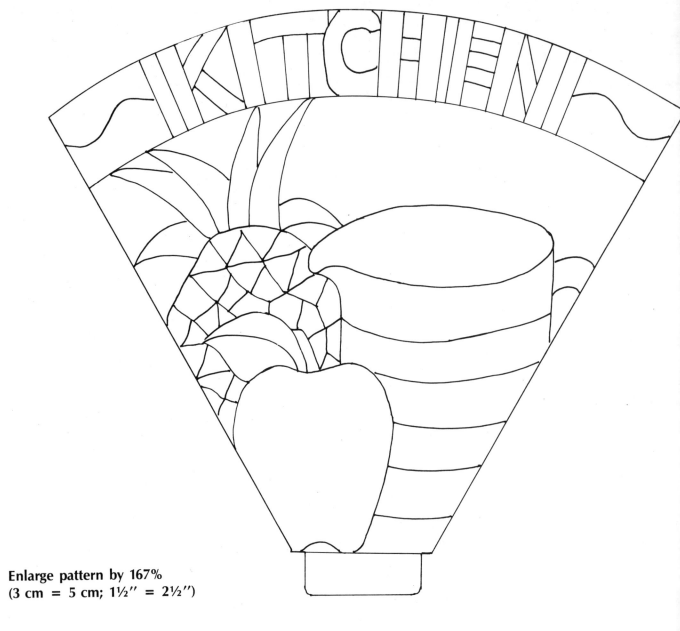

Enlarge pattern by 167%
(3 cm = 5 cm; 1½″ = 2½″)

Tips for coachlamps

1. Foil and solder each of the four panels in a jig. Position and solder square U lead around each panel. Patina and clean.

2. Tin outside edge on both sides of galvanised iron 165 mm (6½'') square lid. Persevere with this. Sand well before tinning and smooth off.

3. Tack-solder four panels into a square as shown in the bird's-eye view. Check with L-square. Solder top, middle and bottom. Then solder lid to panels, solder around edges and smooth off.

4. Twist 5.9R lead approximately twenty-four times. Cut to size, solder into the corners at the top, middle and bottom.

5. Paint lid with flat black rustguard, clean and polish all over.

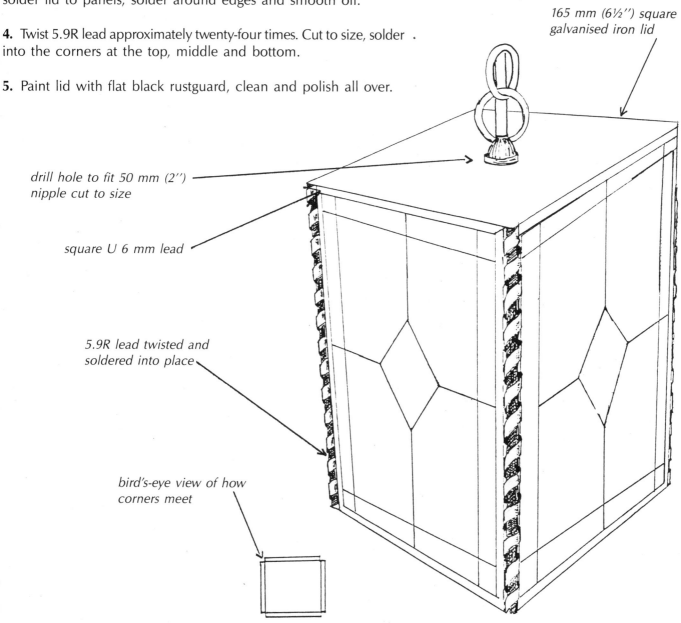

165 mm (6½'') square galvanised iron lid

drill hole to fit 50 mm (2'') nipple cut to size

square U 6 mm lead

5.9R lead twisted and soldered into place

bird's-eye view of how corners meet

Ludbrook's coachlamp

Illustrated on page 45

Pattern actual size

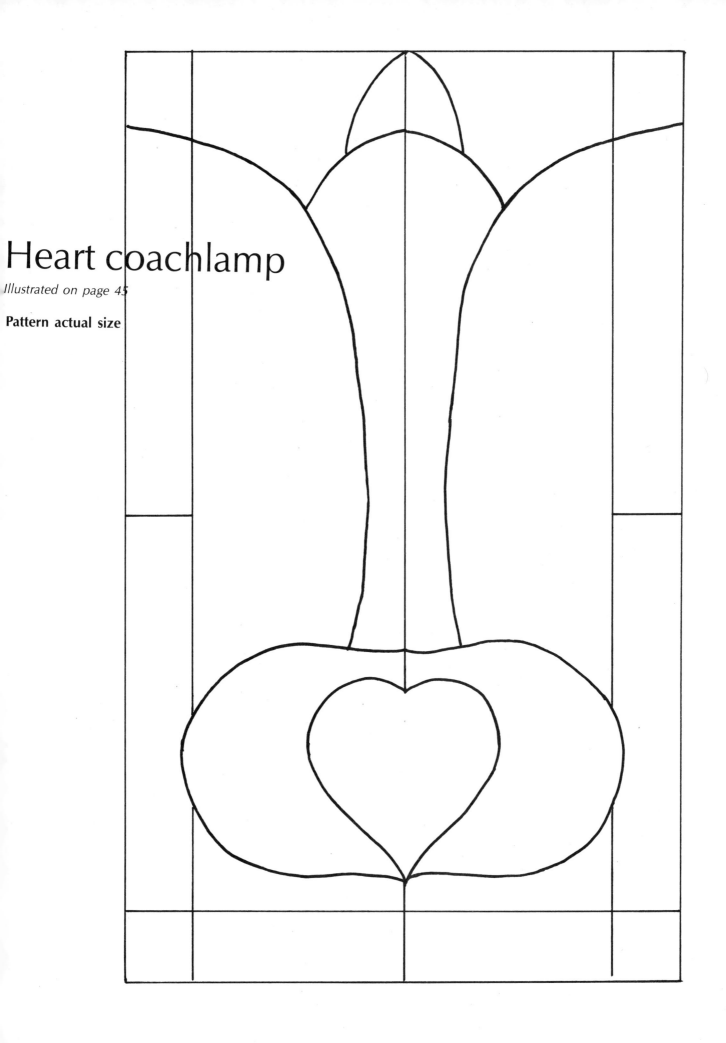

Heart coachlamp

Illustrated on page 45

Pattern actual size

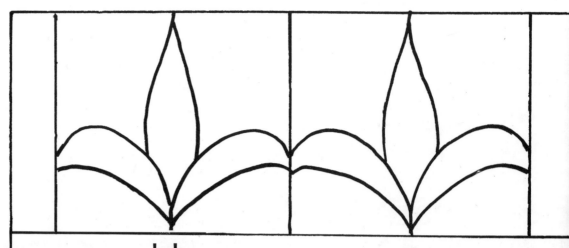

Sunflower coachlamp

Pattern actual size

MIRRORS

Tips for leadlight mirrors

1. Treat mirror glass as leadlight glass, but be very careful that you don't scratch the silver off the back of it. Score on front of mirror, cut on a towel and shake off any slivers of glass.

2. I will only make mirrors with lead around the mirror itself. If any fine work needs to be done, do that in foil, but never surround mirror with foil as the solder used eats into the silver backing. When soldering mirrors, use tallow candle. Scrub joints with wire brush before rubbing on candle.

3. Opaque glass is used for mirrors unless it will be hung in a window, when clear glass is totally acceptable. If you're desperate to use clear glass in a framed mirror then place white paper behind the mirror before adding ply backing.

4. Black solder joints   To make black solder joints, putty, trim, then scrub with bristle brush and a small amount of whiting. The more you scrub the better. Apply stove-black polish sparingly with toothbrush and lightly buff. If joints become silver again, scrub again with hard brush. Do this as soon as you have soldered the panel or mirror.

Note: If you really want to foil around mirrors, apply nail varnish or a recommended paint from a glass supplier around the edges, and use non-toxic flux (Laco or tallow candle). Make a sample and let it sit for a month or so, then check for black spots on mirror.

Floral mirror

Illustrated on page 46

Foiled with lead around mirror and
U6 around complete mirror.
Solder border in large chunks, fit them
around the mirror, then solder together
completely.

Enlarge pattern by 167%
(3 cm = 5 cm; 1½″ = 2½″)

Fuchsia lamp (page 34)

*Old-fashioned
butterfly lamp
(page 37)*

Ludbrook's coachlamp (page 40)

Heart coachlamp (page 41)

Floral mirror (page 44) and small shell mirror (page 49)

Waratah and flannel flower mirror (page 50)

Sunflowers mirror (page 52)

Art Deco rose mirror (page 54)

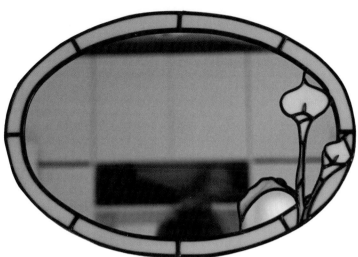

Arum lilies mirror (page 56)

Beach scene mirror (page 58)

Tulips mirror (page 60)

Rose arbour mirror (page 62)

Black and white Art Deco mirror (page 64)

Included just for fun...a hanging panel, one of my favourite pieces

Small shell mirror

Illustrated on page 46

Cut and lead up mirror, solder, putty, polish. Foil shells, tin and then wash flux off. Flux lead where shells will meet and tack-solder. (You might have to scratch the surface a little with your lead knife so that shells will tack-solder successfully.)

Enlarge pattern by 125%
(4 cm = 5 cm; 2″ = 2½″)

Waratah and flannel flower mirror

Illustrated on page 46

Approx. 410 mm (16¼'') diameter.
Foil all of the bottom flowers, leaves
and background. Solder into one
piece, then lead up whole panel,
pushing any foil that might be
obvious back under lead. Lead
around *all* mirror.

join

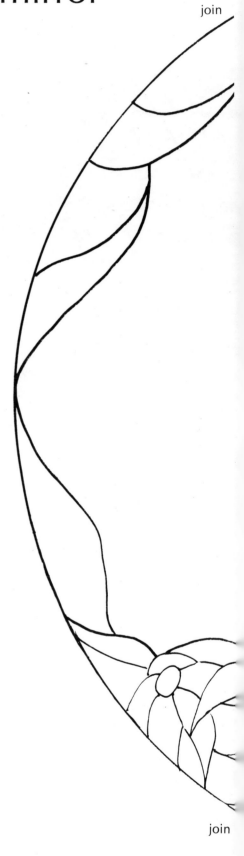

join

50

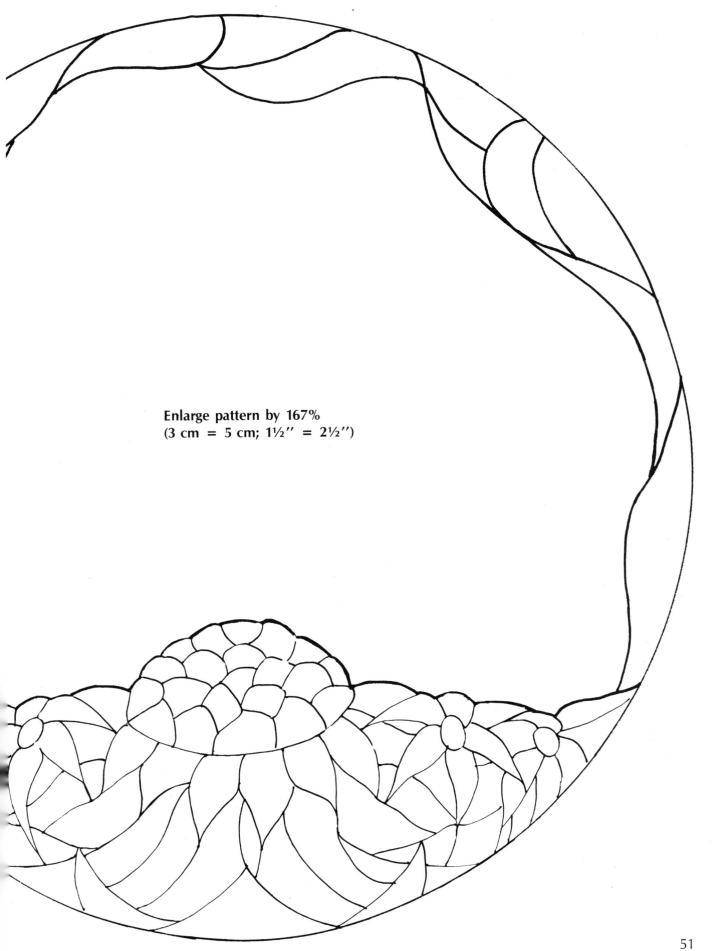

Enlarge pattern by 167%
(3 cm = 5 cm; 1½″ = 2½″)

Sunflower mirror

Illustrated on page 46

Approx. 430 mm × 355 mm
(17'' × 14'')

Foil sunflowers and solder. Lead up the rest of the mirror, fitting sunflowers in place and soldering to lead. Solder copper wire rings securely to the back to hang.

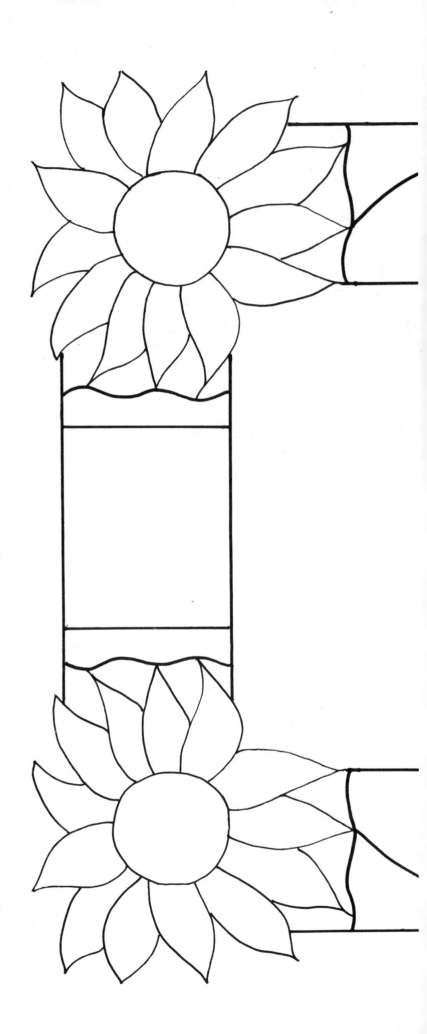

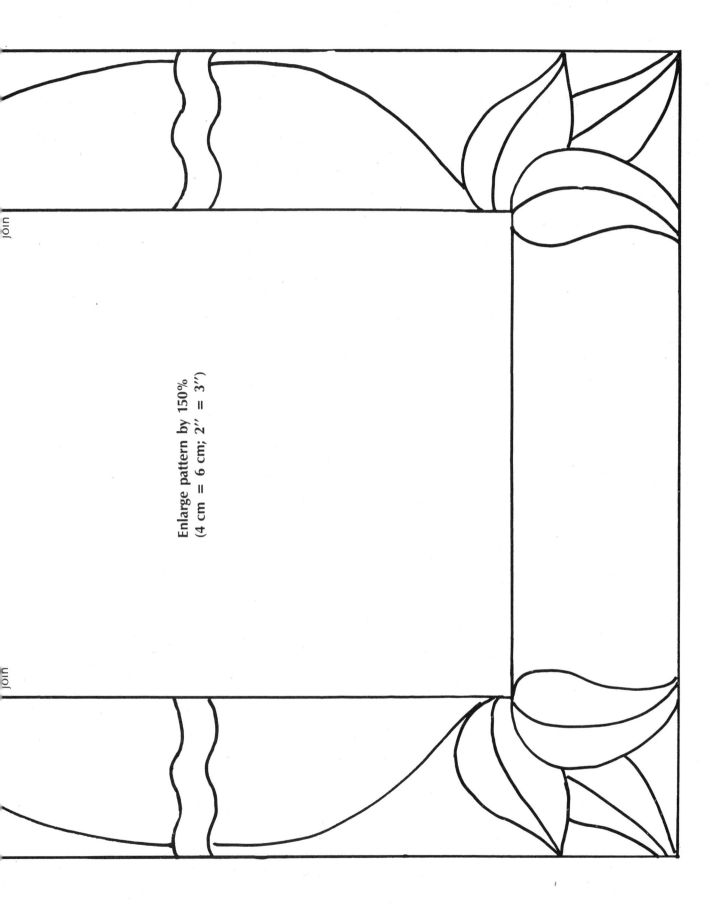

join

join

Enlarge pattern by 150%
(4 cm = 6 cm; 2″ = 3″)

Art Deco rose mirror

Illustrated on page 47

Approx. 775 mm × 390 mm
(30½″ × 15¼″)

There are many colour possibilities for this mirror, and because of its size the mirror looks impressive. This mirror would also go well hanging horizontally.

join

join

Enlarge pattern by 200%
(3 cm = 6 cm; 1½" = 3")

Arum lilies mirror

Illustrated on page 47

Approx. 540 mm × 370 mm
(21¼″ × 14½″)

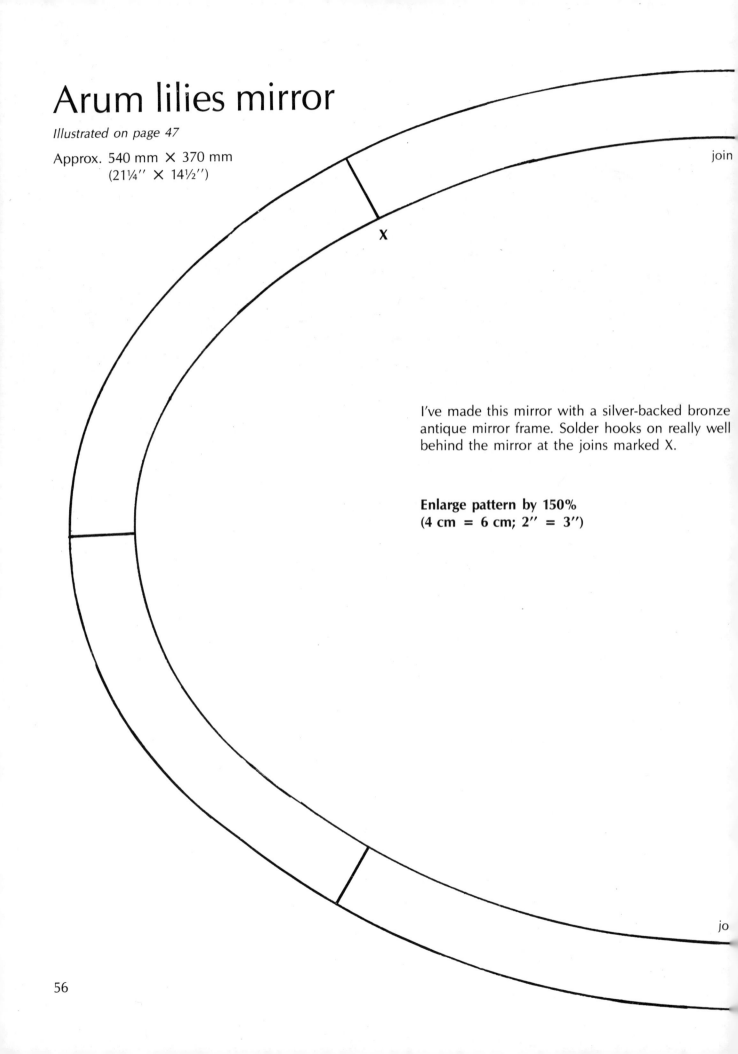

join

X

I've made this mirror with a silver-backed bronze antique mirror frame. Solder hooks on really well behind the mirror at the joins marked X.

**Enlarge pattern by 150%
(4 cm = 6 cm; 2″ = 3″)**

jo

56

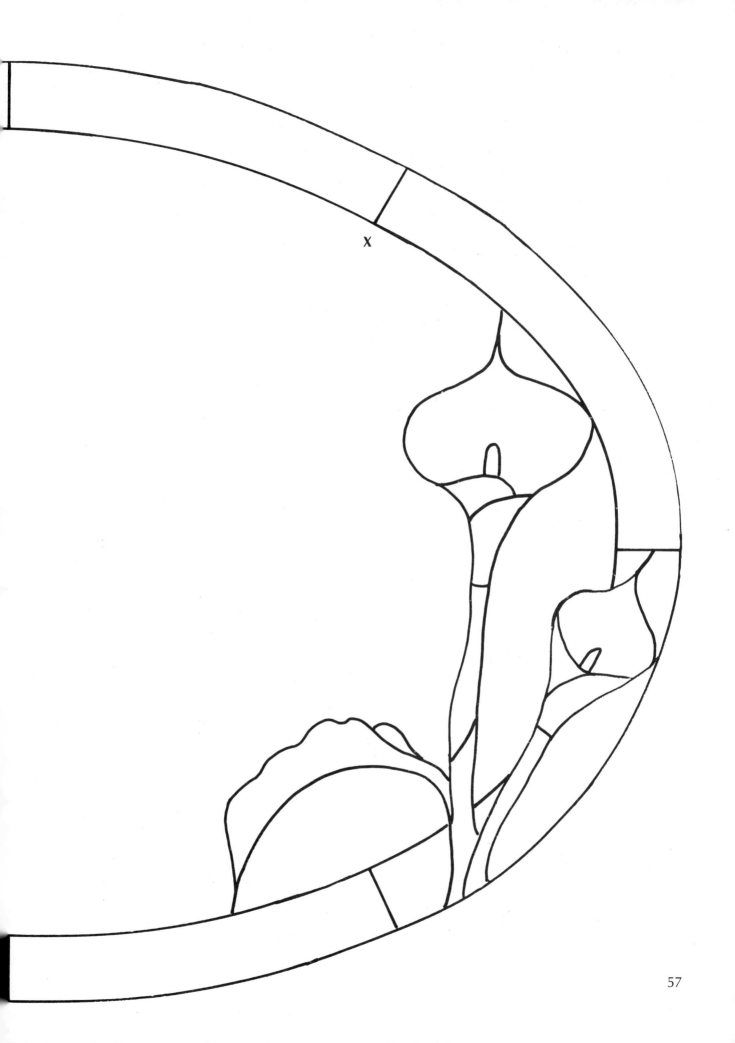

X

Beach scene mirror

Illustrated on page 47

Approx. 420 mm (16½") diameter
Solder a small piece of copper wire
to lead to make tip of umbrella.
Solder hooks behind mirror at spots
marked X.

Enlarge pattern by 167%
(3 cm = 5 cm; 1½" = 2½")

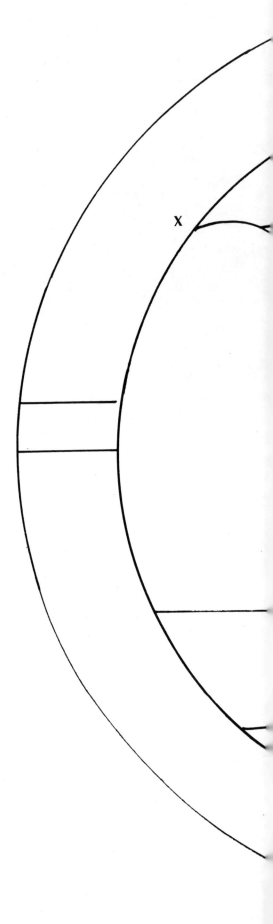

join

X

join

Tulips mirror

Approx. 725 mm × 590 mm
(28½'' × 23¼'')

This large mirror is very popular. Framing with timber sets it off well.

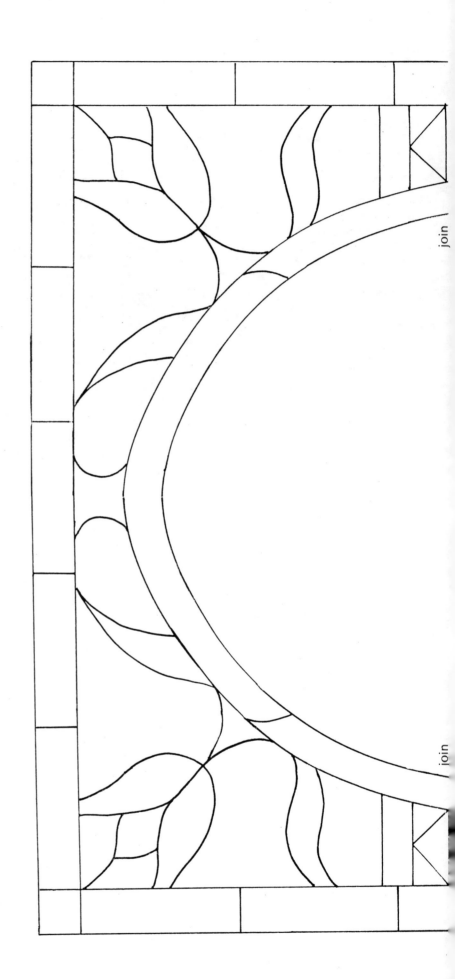

join

join

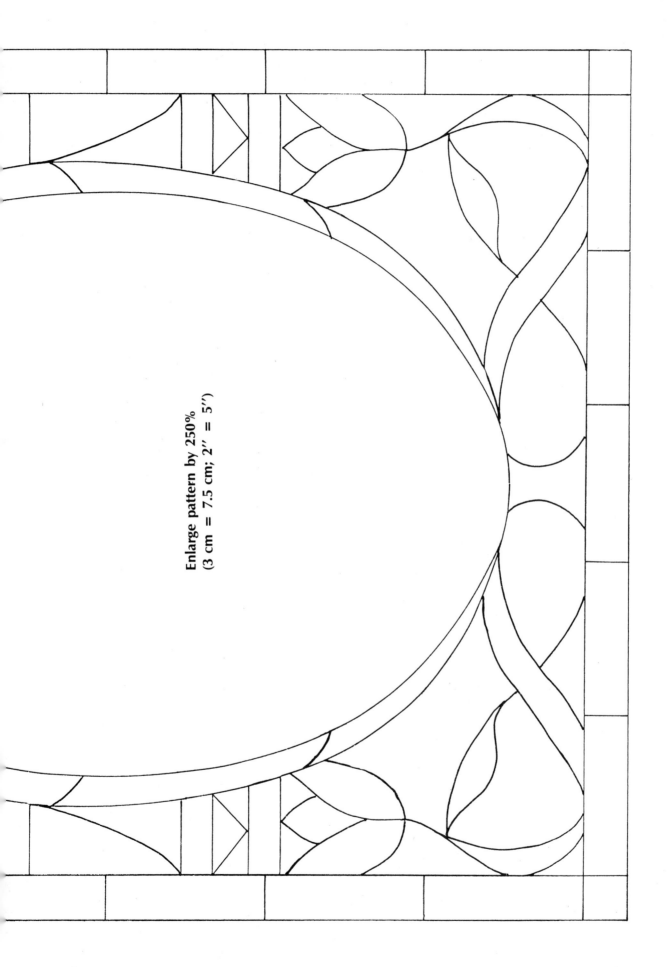

Enlarge pattern by 250%
(3 cm = 7.5 cm; 2″ = 5″)

61

Rose arbour mirror

Illustrated on page 48

Approx. 610 mm × 422 mm
(24" × 16½")

I found this mirror hard to lead up. I used 3.2R and 4.2R lead around the leaves and flowers. It turned out looking great but what a fiddly job—it took 7 hours to lead up. I would enlarge this to about 815 mm × 560 mm (32" × 22") if I did it again.

join

join

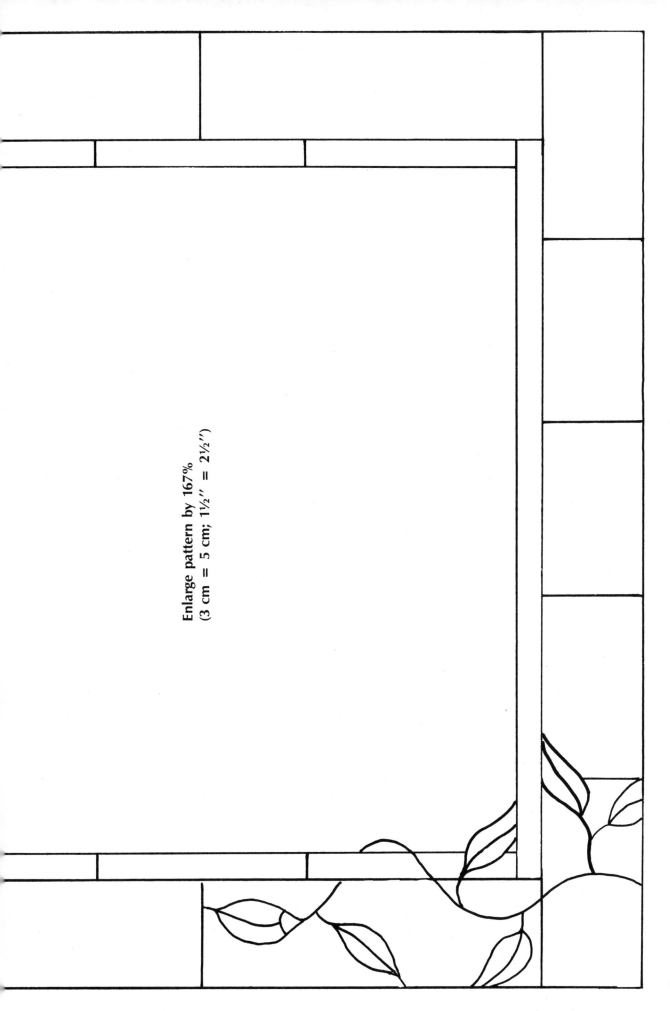

Enlarge pattern by 167%
(3 cm = 5 cm; 1½″ = 2½″)

Black and white Art Deco mirror

Illustrated on page 48

Approx. 475 mm × 312 mm
(18¾″ × 12¼″)

A simple mirror which doesn't need the added expense of a frame.
U6 around outside edge.
Using silvered antique mirror glass adds to the Art Deco style.

Enlarge pattern by 125%
(4 cm = 5 cm; 2″ = 2½″)

Bamboo mirror

Approx. 612 mm ✕ 360 mm
(24″ ✕ 14″)
This mirror should be framed for strength.

Enlarge pattern by 150%
(4 cm = 6 cm; 2″ = 3″)

Gothic mirror

This Gothic mirror is one of my favourites. Unfortunately it was sold before I had taken a good photo of it. I chose to do the whole mirror in mirror glass and the lead lines really make it. It was framed with an olive-green frame and looked great.

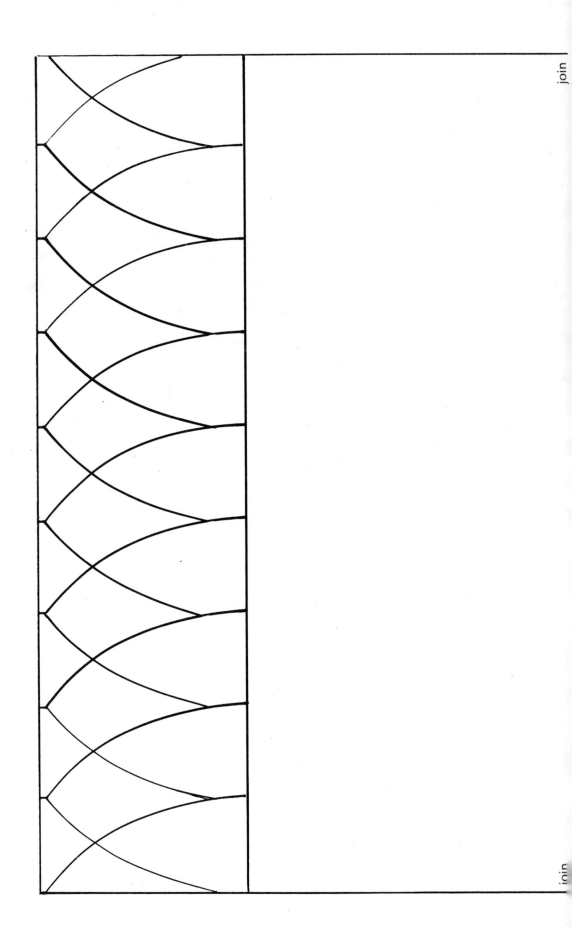

join

join

Enlarge pattern by 200%
(3 cm = 6 cm; 1½″ = 3″)

Cottage buds mirror

Approx. 620 mm × 300 mm
(24½″ × 12″)
This simple mirror was designed for my students. It looks great over a sideboard. One student made it with an opal blue waterglass background, green leaves and yellow buds. Endless colour combinations are possible.

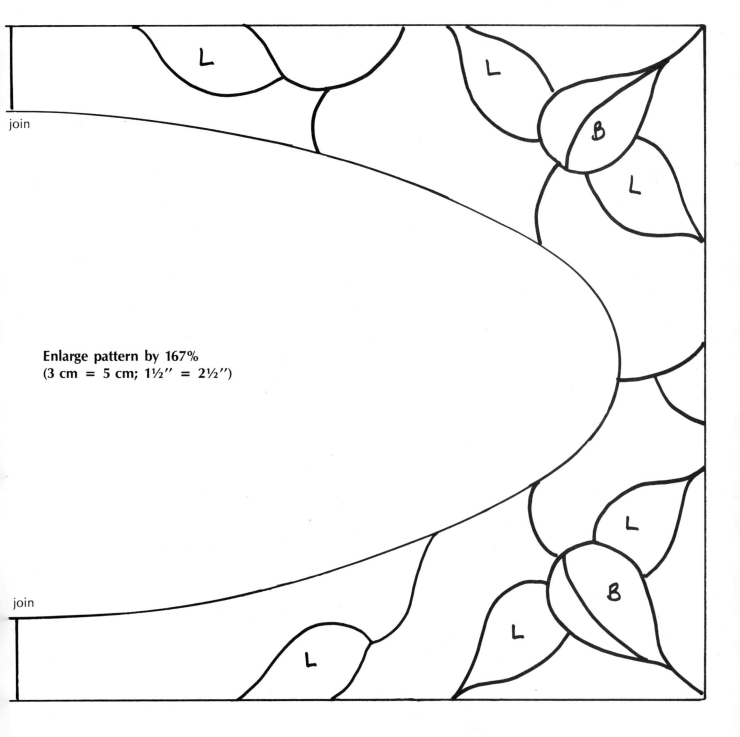

join

Enlarge pattern by 167%
(3 cm = 5 cm; 1½″ = 2½″)

join